Canterbury College
D0272772
156343

ANIMAL FAMILIES

Penguins

angus

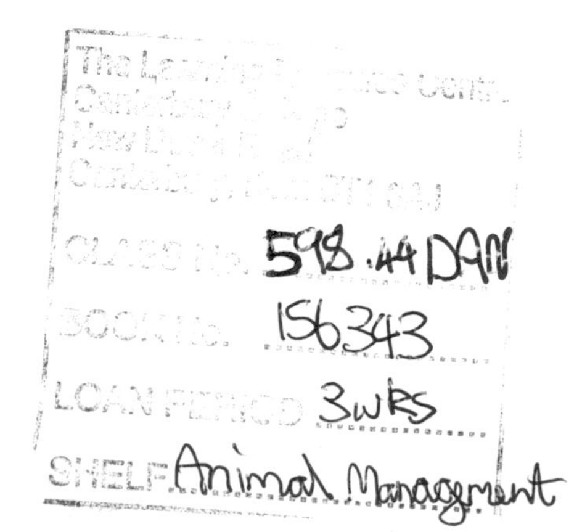

This edition published in 2004
by Angus Books Ltd
12 Ravensbury Terrace
London SW18 4RL

ISBN 1-904594-57-3

© 2001 Brown Partworks Limited.

All rights reserved. Except for use in a review, no part of this book may be reproduced, stored in a retrieval system, or transmitted in any form, or by any means, electronic, mechanical photocopying, recording, or otherwise, without prior permission of the publisher or copyright holder.

All rights reserved. Except for use in a review, no part of this book may be reproduced, stored in a retrieval system, or transmitted in any form, or by any means, electronic, mechanical photocopying, recording, or otherwise, without prior permission of the publisher or copyright holder.

FOR BROWN PARTWORKS LIMITED
Author: Daniel Gilpin
Consultant: Dr. Adrian Seymour
Project editor: Tim Harris
Managing editor: Anne O'Daly
Picture research: Adrian Bentley
Index: Margaret Mitchell

PICTURE CREDITS
Artworks: AntBits Illustration

Adrian Bentley: 28. Ardea London: (Graham Robertson) 12. *Bruce Coleman Collection*: (Allan G. Potts) 7 below, 8; (Dr Eckart Pott) 14, 21 below, 26–27; (Gunter Ziesler) 11; (Hans Reinhard) 16, 17 above; (Johnny Johnson) front cover, 4, 5 above, 27; (Rinie van Meurs) 23 above. *Corbis*: (Kevin Schafer) 29 above; (Wolfgang Kaehler) 13, 15. *NHPA*: (A.N.T.) contents page, 17 below; (B. & C. Alexander) 29 below; (Gerard Lacz) title page, 18; (John Shaw) 6, 7 above, 19; (Kevin Schafer) 21 above, 24; (Martin Harvey) 25; (Rod Planck) 5 below, 10. *Still Pictures*: (Christophe Guinet) 22; (Mark Carwardine) 23 below.

Series created by Brown Partworks Limited.
Designed by Wilson Design Associates

Production by Omnipress,
Eastbourne, UK
Printed and bound in Dubai

Contents

Introduction

Penguins are among the most familiar and best loved of any wild birds. All live in the southern hemisphere, and some inhabit Antarctica, the world's coldest continent.

There are 17 different species (types) of penguins, including the king penguin, emperor penguin, Adelie penguin, and fairy penguin. The most northerly penguins are found close to the equator, but far more live in the icy wastes of Antarctica. Penguins cannot fly, and they waddle clumsily on land; but in the sea they are expert swimmers. In short bursts they can "fly" through the water at speeds of up to 20 mph (32km/h).

Penguins are sociable birds that do most things in groups, especially in the breeding season.

▼ Waiting to take the plunge: Adelie penguins breed on the coast of Antarctica and hunt near the edge of the pack ice for the rest of the year. When they are not in the sea, they can often be seen riding on icebergs floating offshore.

▼ *Macaroni penguin partners greet each other with a calling display as they swap egg-sitting duties.*

What's in a name?

Some types of penguins have been given more than one common name. For example, the chinstrap penguin is also sometimes known as the ringed penguin or the bearded penguin. This can become very confusing.

To simplify matters, scientists give all animals and plants a scientific name, which never changes. This avoids any confusion for people from different countries, who may not use the same common name for the same species. For example, the chinstrap penguin's scientific name is *Pygoscelis antarctica*.

A place where large numbers of penguins breed is called a colony or rookery. Some of them are huge: More than two million macaroni penguins breed on one small island.

Why do penguins get together in these enormous colonies? And why do they do other things in groups? In this book you will find the answers to these questions. You will also discover more about these fascinating birds, including where they live and how they bring up their babies.

► *These king penguins look slightly comical as they waddle across a beach.*

Why penguins live in groups

Penguins live in groups for one main reason—there is safety in numbers. A group of penguins is more likely to spot a lurking predator than a lone bird is. An individual penguin fleeing a predator as part of a group is less likely to get caught than it would be if it was swimming alone.

Penguins breed in colonies because it gives their chicks a better chance of survival. Penguin groups have no real social structure. In many ways they are like shoals of fish—every bird is equal, and there are no leaders.

But unlike fish, penguins have times when they need their own space. Penguins nesting in colonies are almost always evenly spread out and out of pecking reach of one another.

A few penguins live in groups for more than just protection

▼ ***Penguins often establish their colonies on the coast so they do not have to travel a long way from the sea with food for the chicks.***

▲ These penguins are "porpoising," or jumping clear out of the water as they swim.

from predators. Male emperor penguins huddle together during the freezing Antarctic winters to keep themselves warm. Some scientists also think that penguins may hunt more efficiently in groups than on their own, although this is difficult to prove.

Time for a change

Once a year every penguin must change its feathers. This change is called moulting. A moult takes between two and six weeks. It starts from several weeks to several months after the breeding season, depending on the species. Moulting penguins cannot swim or hunt for fish, so they fatten themselves up as much as they can before the process begins. While they are waiting for their new feathers to grow, they may lose up to half their body weight.

▼ A penguin looks scruffy when it is moulting its old feathers.

Hunting and fishing

Like most seabirds, penguins live mainly on a diet of fish and krill, tiny shrimplike crustaceans that often swarm in huge numbers. The larger penguin species also dive for squid.

▼ Long, pointed beaks are an adaptation for these king penguins to grab their squid prey.

Penguins are well adapted for hunting their slippery prey. They are fast and agile swimmers that can twist and turn to follow the movements of fleeing shoals

Distance swimmers and deep-sea divers

All penguins eat the same basic kinds of food, but some go to greater lengths than others to get it. The greatest travellers are emperor penguins. They may stay at sea for as long as a month and travel as far as 950 miles (1,500km) from their breeding grounds in search of food. They also perform some truly remarkable dives. One emperor penguin was recorded diving to 1,752 ft (535m) below the surface for a meal.

▼ ***Emperor penguins can dive to great depths and stay under water for up to 18 minutes.***

of fish. Penguins' eyes are well adapted for the underwater environment, and some penguins have better vision in the water than on dry land. Their white belly may act as camouflage, hiding the penguins from fish in the water below. Like other birds, penguins have no teeth, but they do have tough spikes on their tongue and the roof of their mouth. These spikes are ideal for grasping slippery fish.

A penguin's favorite food is reflected in the size and shape of its beak. King and emperor penguins hunt mainly squid, and they have long, pincerlike beaks to snap up their long-bodied, fast-moving prey. Smaller penguins that eat more krill or fish have shorter, stubbier bills.

Considering their size, penguins can consume huge quantities of food. One Magellanic penguin was found to have eaten almost 9 pounds (4kg) of squid in a single hunt. The average weight of a Magellanic penguin with an empty stomach is just 11.5 pounds (about 5kg), so this bird had almost doubled its weight. On the other hand, penguins are very good at getting through the lean times. When they are moulting, and so unable to hunt, most species survive for weeks on end without food.

Built to grip

► ***A penguin's tongue has spikes for holding fish.***

Breeding time

With the exception of one species, penguins breed once a year. Most gather at their nesting colonies in late spring to mate and lay their eggs, rearing their young so they are ready to swim by the summer.

A few species do things differently, however. Emperor penguins incubate their eggs through the winter. Those that live further north, for example macaroni, rockhopper, and fairy penguins, start breeding in the middle of winter so that their chicks are ready to go to sea in late spring.

The real odd one out is the king penguin. Its chicks take up to 16 months to grow, so the adults can only breed at best

▼ ***This pair of rockhopper penguins is strengthening its partnership with a show of mutual grooming.***

To build or not to build

Most penguins face one main problem when it comes to building a nest, and that is the lack of suitable building material. Some penguins get around this by not making a nest at all. King and emperor penguins balance their eggs on their feet. The Magellanic penguin digs a burrow.

The alternative is usually to build a nest from pebbles or to lay eggs on the bare ground. Some penguins build their nests from grass and other soft material; but because penguins cannot fly, the material has to be available close at hand.

▲ With its beak pointing skyward and wings outstretched, this chinstrap penguin is calling to attract a mate.

twice every three years. As a result, some pair up in spring and others in summer. The following year the early breeders do not get to mate until summer, while the late birds miss out altogether and have to wait for the next spring.

The breeding season is a noisy, bustling time for all penguins. Males usually arrive at the colony first and set about finding the place where they nested the year before. First-time breeders have to grab an empty site or settle on the edge of the colony. The advertising then starts in earnest. Male penguins try to attract females by calling loudly. Eventually almost all of the males have found a mate.

Egg-laying and incubation

Soon after she has paired up and mated, the female penguin lays her eggs. King and emperor penguins lay a single egg. All other penguins lay two.

Penguins lay very small eggs for their body size. The emperor penguin lays the smallest egg of any bird in proportion to its bodyweight.

Brooding in the freezer

Emperor penguins have a really tough time during incubation. While most species spend a few weeks keeping their eggs warm before they hatch, emperors do this for more than two months. The timing of their breeding season means that they incubate during the sunless Antarctic winter, when temperatures can drop as low as –76°F (–60°C), and winds howl at up to 125 mph (200km/h). Only the male emperor penguin incubates.

Cradle snatchers

Nesting penguins have to protect their eggs from would-be thieves. Gulls and other scavenging seabirds, such as skuas and sheathbills, regularly patrol penguin colonies looking for unguarded or abandoned eggs to eat. Small chicks are also vulnerable if they are not watched carefully.

▲ An ever-alert skua seizes an unguarded penguin egg. Sheathbills also steal eggs.

◄ Male emperor penguins do not eat for the two months they are incubating their egg. They may lose half their body weight in this period while the females are feeding at sea.

Its egg tips the scales at just 1.4 percent of the mass of the bird that produced it.

What they lack in size penguin eggs make up for in strength. They have evolved super-thick eggshells, perhaps in response to the adults' clumsiness on land. Weak eggs would not last very long in colonies crowded with clumsy adult penguins.

With the exception of emperor penguins both parents take turns incubating the eggs. The smallest penguins brood for the shortest lengths of time—fairy penguins spend just 33 days sitting before their eggs hatch. The largest penguins take the longest. King penguins brood for 55 days, and emperor penguins' eggs hatch only after 64 days.

Bringing up baby

Penguin chicks hatch from the egg already covered in a fine coat of down but with their eyelids sealed together. They chip through the thick shell with the help of an egg tooth, a short, sharp spike on the end of the beak. The egg tooth drops off soon after hatching.

Growing up

Most penguins catch their food far out to sea, so bringing it back for their chicks is not a simple matter. Rather than risk losing their catch on the way home, they swallow it. When an adult penguin returns from a fishing trip, the young bird reaches into its parent's throat, forcing it to cough up, or regurgitate, the food.

► A chinstrap penguin chick encouraging its parent to regurgitate some fish.

Penguin chicks are hungry from the moment they arrive in the world. Luckily, most emerge to find a ready-made meal of half-digested fish, krill, or squid waiting for them. The parents drop regurgitated balls of food on the egg as it is hatching.

The weeks pass in a constant stream of comings and goings. In most species the mother and father share the duties. One parent keeps the chick warm. The other parent searches for food, only to return, regurgitate its catch, and take over care of the youngster. The cycle continues until the chick is ready to fledge and take to the water. The quickest developers do this at 50 days old.

▲ Chinstrap penguins lay two eggs, but it is unusual for both chicks to survive their difficult first few weeks.

◄ Lacking the thick feathers of their parents, baby penguins can be vulnerable to cold weather. This chick is keeping warm by balancing on its parent's feet.

Emperor penguins will even care for chicks that do not belong to them. If an emperor chick is left alone for a short time by its parents, another adult or an older chick will keep it warm until the parent returns. If an emperor chick hatches before its mother has returned from fishing, the dad can feed it for a while with a curdlike substance he produces.

Although most penguins lay two eggs, it is unusual for more than one chick to survive. The second chick usually starves to death within two weeks of hatching, unable to compete with its larger brother or sister for its parents' attention.

Growing up

The chicks of different penguin species take different lengths of time to reach adult size and lose their downy plumage. They all grow quickly—an Adelie chick grows 14 times bigger in the first two weeks of its life. But for most chicks it is at least two months before they are large enough to look after themselves. In general, the bigger the penguin, the longer this takes.

Penguin chicks are kept under constant guard for the first few weeks of their lives. Even in the Antarctic there are plenty of predators waiting to take advantage of a helpless baby on its own. By the time they are about four weeks old, most chicks start exploring the area around them. Not long after that their parents start to leave them on their own. They continue to feed their young during this "post-guarding stage;" but when the chicks are between two and four months old, the parents abandon them. By this time most chicks have started to lose their fluffy coats and show their adult plumage. They are almost always

◄ Almost as big as its parent, this king penguin chick is still covered in soft, downy feathers. The small bird is a sheathbill, on the lookout for scraps.

► If one chick dies, all the parents' energies can be focused on looking after the survivor. This macaroni penguin is providing shelter from the sun with its wing.

well stocked with fat to carry them through the trials of learning to fish for themselves.

During the postguarding stage many baby penguins find safety in numbers. While their parents are away fishing, the chicks of king, emperor, Adelie, chinstrap, gentoo, and all the crested penguin species gather together in groups known as crêches. By doing this baby penguins are less likely to be picked off by flying predators. In very cold weather they may also huddle together to stay warm.

Late developers

While most penguins stay as chicks for just a few months, the king penguin makes a marathon of it. King penguin chicks do not fledge until they are 10 to 13 months old—almost four times older than most others.

▼ Colonies become huge crêches when the chicks hatch.

The physical penguin

Penguins are highly adapted swimming machines. Their feathers are short and tightly packed to form a smooth covering that offers very little resistance to water. Their wings have become flippers and their feet rudders.

The penguin's body is perfect for moving through water. Its streamlined shape is similar to that of aquatic mammals such as seals, dolphins, and whales. When a penguin is hunting, it makes its body even more streamlined by pulling its head into its shoulders and holding its feet tight against the body.

Penguins have perhaps the most unusual wings of any bird. While most birds' wings are

▲ ***The sleek shape of a swimming penguin looks rather like a whale.***

► ***A penguin's wings are of little use once out of the water.***

designed for flight, penguins' wings are adapted for swimming. Penguins swim by flapping their flattened wings—or flippers—up and down so that they look like they are flying through the water. The wing bones are fused together to make the flippers stiff and strong.

As well as being perfectly built for swimming, penguins are well equipped to keep warm. Their lozenge-shaped bodies have very low surface areas for their weight—they have less skin to lose heat through than most animals their size. Penguins also have a thick layer of fat, or blubber, just under their skin. In fact, most are so well insulated against the cold that they sometimes overheat.

Foot notes

Penguins' feet sit far back on their bodies. When the birds are in the water, their feet act with their tails as rudders to steer them. On land the positioning of the feet makes walking difficult, which accounts for the trademark waddling gait.

The blood vessels inside penguins' feet lie close together to prevent heat loss. Cold blood coming back from the ends of the toes is warmed by hot blood travelling into the feet from the body.

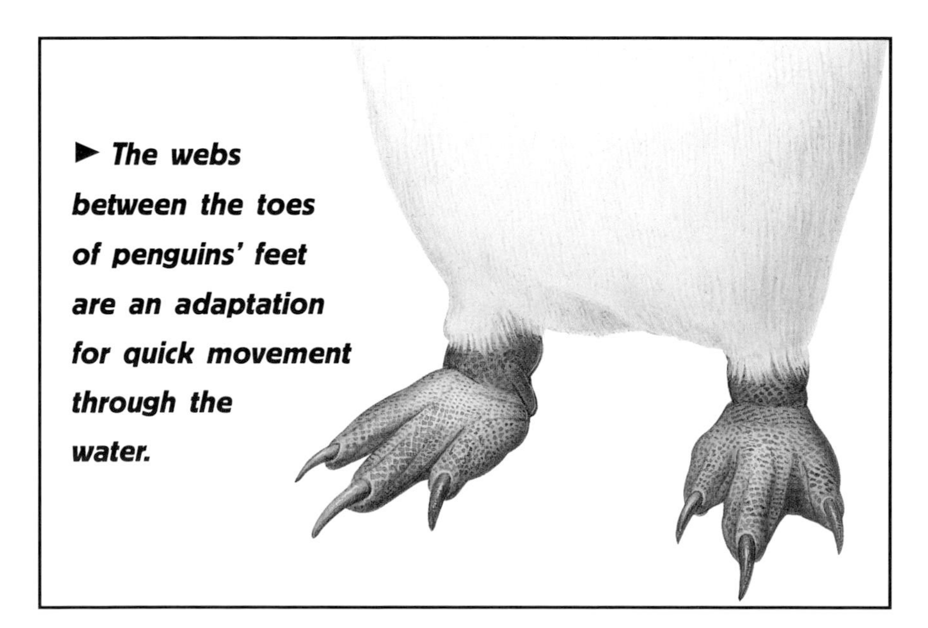

► ***The webs between the toes of penguins' feet are an adaptation for quick movement through the water.***

Penguins past and present

The earliest known penguin fossils are 55 million years old. Scientists think that these flightless birds may have been swimming in the sea as long as 65 million years ago, when the last dinosaurs were still roaming the Earth.

At the same time as the dinosaurs became extinct, so did the giant marine reptiles, leaving a gap in the food chain that penguins were quick to fill. Penguins were at

▲ *Imagine coming face to face with the giant* **Anthropornis nordenskjoeldi,** *known only from its fossil remains.*

Flying cousins

It is strange to think it, but the closest living relatives of penguins include the biggest flying birds alive today. Scientists believe that penguins evolved from the albatross group. Albatrosses are huge seabirds than glide great distances over the oceans in search of fish to eat. The wandering albatross has the largest wingspan of any bird, measuring 11 feet (3.6m) from one wingtip to the other.

their peak from 40 to 25 million years ago. At least 40 types swam the seas, compared with just 17 today. Half of those species were bigger than today's emperor penguin. One of the largest species, *Anthropornis nordenskjoeldi*, stood as tall as a man and may have weighed as much as 300 pounds (135kg).

Apart from two species, penguins today fall into one of four main groups. They are the crested, banded, brush-tail, and large penguins. The exceptions are the yellow-eyed penguin and the fairy penguin.

► All the species of banded penguins, like this Magellanic, have black bands running across their chests.

▼ The gentoo penguin is one of a group of penguins known as the brush-tails.

Dolphin domination

Penguins are highly mobile hunters of fish, krill, and squid in the upper layers of the sea. They were thought to have dominated this environment for millions of years. Their reign may have been brought to an end by the dolphins and toothed whales. As these mammals increased in numbers 20 to 15 million years ago, the larger penguin species may have been unable to compete for food and became extinct.

Penguins' enemies

Wherever they are found, penguins are among the best predators of fish. But penguins themselves feature on the menus of many larger hunters.

In the cold Antarctic waters leopard seals make up as much as 40 percent of their diet from penguins. They mostly attack Adelie, chinstrap, gentoo, and rockhopper penguins. Other seals and sealions also count penguins among their prey. Perhaps the most fearsome penguin predator of all is the killer whale. Pods (groups) of killer whales often swim offshore from penguin colonies, waiting to pluck the snack-sized birds from the water.

Adult penguins have few natural predators outside the sea. Most species nest on remote

▲ Killer whales will often take adult penguins.

► Penguin eggs and young are easy targets for hungry southern giant petrels.

Enemy number one

In Antarctic waters the leopard is the terror of the sea. This leopard is not the spotted big cat most of us are so familiar with, but the leopard seal, a streamlined and efficient predator that rates penguins among its favorite meals. Leopard seals hunt penguins in a number of ways. Sometimes they follow the shadow of a bird as it walks on thin ice, smashing through to grab it before it even knows what has happened. Sometimes they leap from the sea onto ice floes to snatch resting birds. Other times they lie in wait near the shore to grab penguins as they try to leave the water. A fast-swimming penguin can often escape from a leopard seal, but the seals can easily catch an injured penguin or a youngster.

islands where there are few, if any, mammals. Young penguins and eggs are not so lucky. Penguin colonies are often plagued by airborne killers, such as skuas, giant petrels, and sheathbills. These large seabirds are unable to take adults, but they can take their toll on penguin numbers all the same.

Penguins in strange places

Penguins seem to go with Antarctica like polar bears with the Arctic. But in fact, more than half of the world's penguin species never go near Antarctic waters, and one lives near the equator.

Emperor penguins are hardly ever seen outside the Antarctic, and Adelies are found almost exclusively in the cold waters surrounding the southern continent. Chinstrap and gentoo penguins nest on Antarctica and its surrounding islands but are also found further north. The remainder of the 17 species nest outside the Antarctic circle. Magellanic and Humboldt penguins breed on the shores of South America and its offshore islands. Snares Island, erect-crested, and macaroni penguins have colonies on small islands just south of New Zealand, while yellow-eyed and fairy penguins nest on the shores of New Zealand itself. Fairy penguins

◄ Coastal forests on New Zealand's South Island provide an unlikely home for yellow-eyed penguins.

▲ *Jackass penguins nest in colonies along the coasts of South Africa and Namibia.*

◄ *This map shows places where penguins are found.*

also breed around Tasmania and on southern coasts of Australia.

Two species of penguin are found in very unlikely places. The Galápagos penguin inhabits the islands from which it gets its name, not far from the equator.

The Fjordland penguin has perhaps the strangest nesting grounds of any species. This crested penguin brings up its chicks in the temperate rainforests of islands off southwestern New Zealand.

Penguins on the equator

The most northerly penguins of all live in the Galápagos islands, a group of islands in the Pacific Ocean that straddles the equator. Galápagos penguins thrive on fish fed by the nutrient-rich Cromwell current that washes around the islands. Every few years this current fails; and when this happens, many penguins starve. In 1984 numbers fell dramatically from several thousand to just 463 birds, though they have recovered since.

Habitat

When people think of penguins, they usually picture them in frozen wastes or on the rocky coasts and islands where most of them breed. But a penguin's real habitat is the open ocean.

The reason that penguins are so clumsy and comical on land is that their bodies are adapted for a life in the water. Watching them swim makes it clear where they are most at home. Penguins can be found in coastal and oceanic waters almost throughout the southern hemisphere south of the tropic of Capricorn. A few species range further north; and as we have already seen, one species—the Galápagos penguin—lives right on the equator.

Wherever penguins are found on land, they are never very far from the sea. Even emperor

▲ ***Penguins are not fast walkers: they can move more efficiently on ice and snow by "skating" on their bellies.***

Going underground

Galápagos, jackass, Humboldt, Magellanic, and fairy penguins have an added element to their life on land. As well as spending time on the surface, they spend some of it underground. These five species nest in burrows, which they dig themselves. Most burrows are used year after year, and some are decades old. Where the ground is unsuitable for digging, as in many parts of the Galápagos penguin's range, rock crevices are used instead.

Island life

A few species of penguin nest on continental shores, but the majority prefer remote oceanic islands. These far-flung specks of land provide much safer environments for bringing up chicks because few of them have any land-based predators. Jackass penguins, which breed on the South African mainland, have to put up with attacks from mongooses, while Humboldt and magellanic penguins suffer from predation by South American foxes and Geoffroy's cats. Most penguins that choose the island life only have other birds to deal with.

► ***Penguins seem to be better at catching their prey if they go fishing as a group. A collection of penguins on the surface is called a raft.***

penguins overwintering far from the water's edge are closer to the ocean than they realize. In winter much of the ocean around Antarctica freezes, and the "land" that the emperors spend months incubating their eggs on is actually a shelf of ice floating on the seawater underneath.

Penguins and people

Like most creatures on Earth, penguins have suffered hard at the hands of people over the years. The first European explorers to come across them in the late 15th century saw them as easy meat and killed thousands for food.

Later encounters were even more disastrous. In 1775 Captain James Cook reported the existence of huge breeding colonies of fur seals on the beaches of South Georgia in the Falkland Islands. The following century saw the decimation of these colonies, as well as those of the elephant seals that lived around the islands. Penguins were killed in huge numbers to provide fuel for the boiling pots used to extract lard from the slaughtered elephant seals. Later, as the seals began to disappear, penguins themselves were boiled for their lard.

Nowadays few, if any, penguins are killed deliberately by people, but they still die as a result of

◄ ***Penguins have long been very popular attractions in zoos.***

The rarest penguin

Despite the many pressures that penguins face because of people, the numbers of most species are relatively stable. One exception is the yellow-eyed penguin. This handsome bird lives on New Zealand's South Island and a few smaller islands offshore. Its population has plummeted to just over 1,400 breeding pairs in the last few decades as the coastal forests it nests in have been cleared. Introduced predators, such as ferrets and cats, have also had an impact, stealing eggs and killing chicks. Today the yellow-eyed penguin is protected, and its habitat is slowly being restored. Nevertheless, there is a long way to go before the species can be considered out of risk.

► As dense forest has been cleared, yellow-eyed penguins have been forced to nest in more open woodland and scrub.

human activity. Oil spillages from ships and leaking pipelines along the coasts of South America kill tens of thousands of Magellanic and Humboldt penguins every year, and overfishing affects penguin populations almost everywhere. Another problem, and one that is increasing, is the effect of human presence on breeding penguins. One study has shown that increased tourist activity around Adelie penguin colonies leads to fewer chicks being raised successfully. Many disturbed penguins lose eggs and chicks to predators, such as skuas and sheathbills, and some desert their nests completely.

▼ Penguins can tolerate people—if they keep their distance.

Further reading

Handbook of Birds of the World
by J. del Hoyo, A. Elliott, and J. Sagartal (Lynx Edicions, 1992).

Looking at Penguins
by Dorothy Hinshaw Patent and Graham Robertson (Holiday House, 1993).

Mitsuaki's Penguins
by Mitsuaki Iwago (Chronicle Books, 1997).

Penguin
by Frank Staub and Lynn Stone (Early Bird Nature Books, 1998).

Penguins
by Sheila Buff (Nature's Window, 1997).

Penguins
by John A. Love (World Life Library, 1997).

Penguins
by Claire Robinson (Heinemann, 1997).

Penguins
by John Bonnett Wexo (Zoo Books, 1989).

Web Sites

www geocities. com
www.libsci.sc.edu
www.nerc-bas.ac.uk
www.octopus.gma.org
www.scrtec.org

Glossary

Antarctic circle: the line of latitude at 66.5^0 south.

blubber: the layer of fat lying below the skin of penguins and marine mammals.

colony: the place where large numbers of birds come together to lay eggs and raise their young.

crêche: a group of young animals looked after by adults.

crustacean: aquatic invertebrates that form an important part of a penguin's diet.

down: a baby bird's soft, warm feathers.

extinct: an animal that is found alive nowhere on Earth.

flipper: a flat, broad limb that helps a penguin swim through water.

groom: clean and tidy the plumage of another bird.

incubate: sit on eggs to keep them warm, allowing the embryo inside to develop.

krill: the small shrimplike crustaceans found in ocean waters that form an important food source for penguins and other marine animals.

moult: change one set of feathers for another. Penguins do it every year.

plumage: the feathers that grow on a bird's body.

predator: an animal that kills and feeds on other animals.

regurgitate: vomit up partially digested food that chicks find easier to swallow.

squid: fast-moving marine mollusks with tentacles, a torpedo-shaped body, and triangular tail fins.

Index